From This Day Forward

Presented to:

Bruce + Carol

On the occasion of:

Your Wedding

Date:

January 15, 2000

With love from:

Vicky Hayes

LITTLE GIRLS' DREAMS

Childhood wonder upon her face

Visions of flowers, cake, and lace

White horses, picket fences, and blue skies

Long ago dreams in a little girl's eyes.

SUSAN WALES

This book is dedicated to our parents

the late SENATOR MARSHALL WILLIAMS *& his beloved wife* MARGARET WILLIAMS
&
MR. & MRS. ARTHUR HUEY, JR.
What a wonderful example of marriage you are to us

The designer would like to dedicate this book to

CLAUDIA
My wife and closest friend

and to HAYLEY
My little sister who will soon be a Mrs.

Some of the stories in this book are true, and others, while based on true stories, have had certain names and details changed in order to protect the privacy of the individuals.

FROM THIS DAY FORWARD
published by Multnomah Publishers, Inc.

© 1999 by Susan Huey-Wales and Ann Williams-Platz
International Standard Book Number: 1-57673-584-2

Cover and interior photos by Claudia Kunin
Design and illustration by Kirk DouPonce
Photo of flowers on p. 10 and photo of wedding rings on p. 13 by Photodisc
Photo of couple in snow on p. 31 by Rob Johns/Tony Stone Images

Scripture quotations are from *The Holy Bible*, New International Version (NIV) © 1973, 1984
by International Bible Society, used by permission of Zondervan Publishing House.

Also quoted: New American Standard Bible (NASB) © 1960, 1977
by the Lockman Foundation.

Multnomah is a trademark of Multnomah Publishers, Inc., and is registered
in the U.S. Patent and Trademark Office.
The colophon is a trademark of Multnomah Publishers, Inc.

Printed in Hong Kong

For information:
MULTNOMAH PUBLISHERS, INC.•POST OFFICE BOX 1720•SISTERS, OREGON 97759

99 00 01 02 03 04 05 — 10 9 8 7 6 5 4 3 2 1

From This Day
FORWARD

Reflections on Marriage

Susan Wales & Ann Platz

Multnomah Publishers *Sisters, Oregon*

CONTENTS

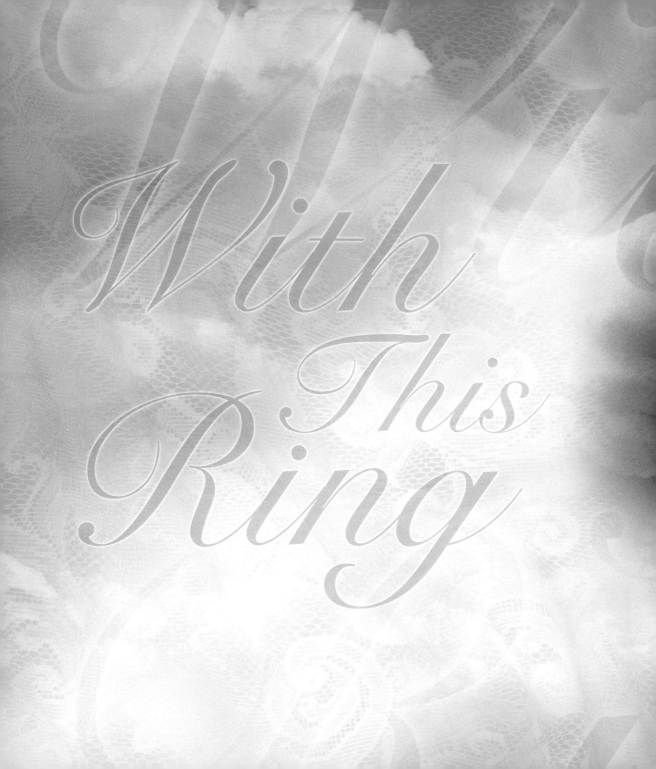

This ring has no beginning and no end,

A symbol of eternal commitment,

A token of my love for you.

It is a

physical,

visible

symbol of an

invisible

reality.

Larry Libby

It is the most subtle of weights on the third finger of the left hand, barely even felt until consciously remembered. And then...there it is, the slightest touch of smooth metal on skin. The soft, yet persistent reminder that life is forever different. A decision has been made. A corner has been turned. Vows have been uttered before the listening ears of heaven. Two lives have been irrevocably linked, flesh to flesh, heart to heart, soul to soul. With simple eloquence, the ring says, "I am wed. I have a life companion. I belong to someone else. My heart, my passion, the deepest reservoirs of my affection are the property of a dear person who means more to me than life itself.

The soft, yet persistent

reminder that life is

forever different.

HIDDEN TREASURES

∞

I have been here before,
But where or how I cannot tell;
I know the grass beyond the door,
The sweet keen smell,
The sighing sound,
the lights around the shore.

<small>DANTE GABRIEL ROSSETTI</small>

Growing up, Leslie had always been a tomboy at heart. She loved to play ball with the neighborhood boys. But because of her tall, slender build, sometimes they picked on her, calling her names like "Beanpole," "Olive Oil," and "Bird Legs."

Michael, a cute boy with dark eyes and hair, was different. He lived next door, and he didn't call Leslie names. In fact, he seemed to adore everything about her. One day when he was seven, Michael shyly gave Leslie a ring from a Cracker Jack box—and asked her to marry him.

Leslie never forgot his proposal, and for many years she continued to have a mad crush on Michael. In high school he excelled in sports and was popular with the girls. But it was obvious to Leslie that he didn't see his skinny childhood friend as girlfriend material.

During college Leslie lost touch with Michael, and then she learned that he'd been drafted by a professional football team in New York. She wasn't at all surprised when one day she read that he was marrying a well-known fashion model. A twinge of disappointment pinched her heart.

But the sadness didn't last. By the time her ten-year class reunion rolled around, Leslie had blossomed into a stunning beauty herself, and she was married to a wonderful man. When she saw Michael arm in arm with his lovely wife, she was sincerely happy for him. Everything had turned out as it should, she decided. *Childhood crushes are for kids, after all. Then you grow up and move on.*

Little did Leslie know that life was about to take a tragic turn. A few years after the reunion, her husband was killed in a plane crash. She had found love—only to have it snatched away.

Engulfed for some time in her grief, Leslie was out of touch with most of her friends by the time her twentieth reunion rolled around. As she mingled, she couldn't help but notice that hardship had visited many of her old acquaintances—including Michael. What her friends had told her was true. He, too, was alone, his wife having died of breast cancer years before.

At the reunion she and Michael cautiously began to renew their friendship. Michael had recently taken a job as an assistant coach for a professional football team. Soon they began to see one another regularly, and Leslie felt sure they were falling in love.

As months turned into years, however, Leslie began to wonder if Michael would ever want to marry her. Maybe she would forever remain his "best friend"—the girl next door.

One night the couple attended a Braves game together. The team was winning, the weather was perfect, and through Michael's great sports connections, they had the best seats in the stadium. After a few innings, Michael excused himself to get snacks. He returned with Cokes and Cracker Jacks.

Leslie smiled, but her eyes grew misty. Obviously Michael didn't recall his childhood Cracker Jack proposal. How silly of her to have treasured the memory—and the ring—all these years.

When she finished munching, she tossed her box into a trash bin behind her.

Michael jumped out of his seat. "Leslie! You didn't even get your prize!" He leaned into the bin to retrieve her box.

"That's okay," she said. "They don't have good prizes in them like they used to when we were kids."

"Wanna bet?" Michael asked. He handed her the half-empty box. When Leslie reached in for her prize, she pulled out an incredibly beautiful engagement ring!

A moment later a message flashed up on the stadium's giant screen. It said, "Leslie, I love you. Will you marry me? Michael."

Friends who attended Michael and Leslie's wedding agreed that Leslie, once called "Bird Legs," had never looked so beautiful. On her left hand sparkled a lovely diamond wedding set, and on her right the ring from the Cracker Jack box Michael had given her in the second grade.

As the groom leaned down to kiss the bride, Leslie's most cherished childhood dream had finally come true.

Some things, like beauty and love, just take a little time.

To love is to place our happiness

in the happiness of another.

GOTTFRIED WILHELM VON LEIBNITZ

Hand and to Hold

Her champion.

Her lover and friend.

Yet if the "holding"

is for a night or a week

or a season, and no

t for life, the comfort will

turn to desolation,

leaving arms emptier

than if they had never

held another at all

LARRY LIBBY

A husband and wife must have each other...and not in a physical sense alone.

When the rest of the world is against him, when his friends turn away, when his bold enterprises and dreams fall into the dust, a man must know that he has his wife. She is there. She is with him. She is for him. She is his.

When a woman's heart is heavy with sorrow, when her confidence ebbs, when doubts and fears fill her thoughts, robbing sleep from her eyes, she must know that she has her husband. Her man. Her protector. Her champion. Her lover and friend.

It can be a lonely world, an indifferent, uncaring world, a world with a hard edge. Yet when a man holds a woman, and a woman holds a man, there is warmth, great comfort, and a deep sense of rightness.

LOOKING FOR LOVE

~

In my loving way, I am molding two hearts.
If they will only wait for Me in my special time,
Wait upon Me, the Master of the seasons of your heart.

DAVID HARBUCK

I had always known I would not marry early. I had too much to accomplish in my career to even think about a husband and children. But by the time I was thirty-one, I'd finished a graduate degree and was achieving career success in my field of education. Learning styles had become my area of specialty. I thought I could master virtually anything I set my mind to.

Except dating.

Suddenly I realized I didn't have a clue about how to have a normal social life. I hadn't really been paying attention. Where would a woman like me find eligible men who shared my values? I didn't frequent bars, and I had lived through enough church-sponsored singles functions for one lifetime.

So who was going to teach the learning expert how to find the right guy?

In the spring of 1985, I read an article about using the classified ads to meet eligible singles with mutual interests and goals. At first I dismissed the idea as totally absurd, but for some reason I remained intrigued. I noticed that most of the men who interested me read the same upscale newspaper, *The Seattle Weekly*. One day, on impulse, I picked up a copy and studied the Person-to-Person section.

A lot of groaning, gasping, and hooting followed, to be sure. But some of the ads struck me. They were like advertising masterpieces in only twenty words. The best ones were creative, clever, and amazingly nonthreatening. I decided to give it a try. After all, I reasoned, I'm not advertising for a husband, just interesting friends—right?

Here's how my ad appeared:

> **Professional SWF**, 31, looking for a man committed to the solid values in life. If you're looking for casual sex, you're not looking for me. If you're interested in a friendship, let's explore the possibilities.

I got twenty-one replies, all from apparently sane, professional, Christian men. I went out with nine of them (lots of free lunches!). I decided I'd struck on the perfect social tool for a performance-oriented career woman. No muss, no waste, and it put me in total control of who came calling. Perfect.

Until I met John. He was man #4. John was an attractive, stimulating man whose interests paralleled mine. We could spend hours talking. He was everything I'd been looking for, as my heart told me right away—and that was the problem. I felt my years-long tight grip on my life slipping away. Suddenly this stubborn, independent, career-oriented woman had let her heart walk right up to the edge of lover's leap and poise to jump.

After our first time together, I wrote in my journal: "Lunch today—I'm seeing him again. I just don't understand what I'm going through. My style promotes independence and variety, and yet here I am thinking how nice it would be to be committed to someone. There's no doubt that my heart feels more than ready to plunge into unknown waters. And me, who can't swim!"

Things happened fast—for both of us. It felt like we'd been walking toward the same destination for years and suddenly realized that this is where we became seat partners. John said we needed at least twelve months of relationship—"We have to experience every holiday together once," he announced—before we made any lifelong commitments. That sounded like an excellent career plan to me.

But my heart didn't cooperate much. In fact, I discovered I was in the middle of a war— between the plan-ful, hard-charging professional I'd become and a heart that seemed to be saying, "Time's up, Cynthia. You've met your match!"

I wrote in my journal: "I do think since he has custody of my heart that I should be entitled to frequent visitation rights. My heart has certainly not lost any time in drawing up the adoption papers. While it's spreading out the documents and handing John the pen, my mind is busily picking them back up and apologizing for the haste."

A few weeks later, John sent me a poem. It read:

> *Do you and I tumble, or stagger, or stumble*
> *Or topple, or just fall in love?*
> *No, it's more like we fit like a ball in a mitt.*
> *And as planned as hand in a glove.*
> *Now for me to suggest that a test of the rest*
> *Of the best "Weekly" writers is due*
> *Would be near-cavalier; never fear: Here, my dear,*
> *Is the man in God's plan just for you.*
> *So if you're not afraid of the staid or delay*
> *And you prayed for a guy all your own,*
> *Slide all doubting aside, ride astride by my side*
> *I'm as near as your ear to the phone.*
> *With love (and apologies to Dr. Seuss!)—JST*

How could I argue with that? I realized that God had known all along what it would take to peel my fingers off my life and make me take that leap. And now I knew that God would help me learn how to swim.

I let go. John and I had a wonderful, two-year courtship and were married in 1987. Not once since then have I had to worry about what my heart is going to do next. Because I relinquished custody of my heart long ago to John Tobias—and love has taken care of all the rest.

CYNTHIA ULRICH TOBIAS

Oh promise me that

someday you and I,

Will take our love together

to some sky

Where we can be alone

and faith renew,

And find the hollows where

those flowers grew.

CLEMENT WILLIAM SCOTT

For memory has painted

this perfect day

with colors that never fade.

CARRIE JACOBS BOND

From this day,

life changes.

From this day,

something new begins.

From this day,

two paths merge into one.

From this day,

the status of a man

and a woman transforms,

until the end of their days.

It begins with a square on a calendar. A line in a date book.

A point in time. A month. A week. A day. An hour. A moment.

At an appointed time, in an appointed place, before chosen witnesses, a ceremony begins. It may be in a church, with spectrum light streaming through stained glass windows. It might be in a sterile office, devoid of trappings, before a sleepy-eyed justice of the peace. It might be in a green field under a wide blue sky, with banners flying in the wind.

A wedding has a Who and a Where. But it also has a When.

And the When says, "From this day forward."

From this day, life changes. From this day, something new begins. From this day, two paths merge into one. From this day, the status of a man and a woman transforms, until the end of their days.

From this day forward. There is motion here. There is a leaving behind of things past, a severing of old ties, old habits, old loyalties, old haunts. On this day, say bride and groom, we step onto a road neither of us have walked before. There will now be two sets of footprints, side by side. Out in the sunlight, two shadows will be cast, blending into one as day follows day.

From this day forward, life begins anew.

A wedding has a Who and a Where.
But it also has a When.
And the When says,
"From this day forward."

LOVE WITHOUT A NET

❦

*Now join your hands
and with your hands your hearts.*

WILLIAM SHAKESPEARE

Anne Morrow was shy and delicate. Butterfly-like. Not dull or stupid or incompetent, just a quiet specimen of timidity.

Her dad was ambassador to Mexico when she met an adventurous young fellow who visited south of the border for the U.S. State Department.

The man was flying from place to place promoting aviation. Everywhere he went he drew capacity crowds. You see, he had just won forty thousand dollars for being the first to cross the Atlantic by air. The strong pilot and the shy princess fell deeply in love.

When she became Mrs. Charles Lindbergh, Anne could have easily been eclipsed by her husband's shadow. She wasn't, however. The love that bound the two together for the next forty-seven years was tough love, mature love, tested by triumph and tragedy alike. They would never know the quiet comfort of being an anonymous couple in a crowd. The Lindbergh name didn't allow that luxury. Her man, no matter where he went, was news, forever in the limelight—clearly a national hero. But rather than becoming a resentful recluse or another nameless face in a crowd of admirers, Anne Morrow Lindbergh emerged to become one of America's most popular authors, a woman highly admired for her own accomplishments.

How? Let's let her give us the clue to the success of her career.

To be deeply in love is, of course, a great liberating force and the most common experience that frees—ideally, both members of a couple in love free each other to new and different worlds. I was no exception to the general rule. The sheer fact of finding myself loved was unbelievable and changed my world, my feelings about life and myself. I was given confidence, strength, and almost a new character. The man I was to marry believed in me and what I could do, and consequently I found I could do more than I realized.

Charles did believe in Anne to an extraordinary degree. He saw beneath her shy surface. He realized that deep in her innermost well was a wealth of wisdom, a profound, untapped reservoir of ability. Within the security of his love she was freed—released—to discover and develop her own capacity, to cultivate her own skills, and to emerge from that cocoon of shyness a beautiful, ever-delicate butterfly whose presence would enhance many lives far beyond the perimeter of her husband's shadow. He encouraged her to do her own kind of flying, and he admired her for it.

We're talking roots and wings. A husband's love that is strong enough to reassure yet unthreatened enough to release. Tight enough to embrace yet loose enough to enjoy. Magnetic enough to hold, yet magnanimous enough to allow for flight—with an absence of jealousy as others applaud her accomplishments and admire her competence. Charles, the secure, put away the net so Anne, the shy, could flutter and fly.

CHARLES R. SWINDOLL

From *Growing Strong in the Seasons of Life* (Grand Rapids, Mich.: Zondervan Publishing House, 1994). Used by permission of the publisher. All rights reserved.

For Better or for Worse

If we had no winter,

the spring would not

be so pleasant;

If we did not sometimes

taste of adversity,

prosperity would not

be so welcome.

ANNE BRADSTREET

arriage is a long journey through a changing landscape. It isn't always scenic. It isn't always pretty. It isn't always fun. It isn't always exciting. Romance may go into hiding. Feelings may lag so many miles behind determination that you wonder if they will ever catch up. But all the while, the road is leading somewhere. Stay on that road, endure the desolate stretches, climb the long hills together, and you will find vistas beyond what you had imagined.

The road to "for better" sometimes travels through "for worse."

And it is worth the journey.

I never knew a night so black

Light failed to follow in its track.

I never knew a storm so gray

It failed to have its clearing day.

I never knew such bleak despair

That there was not a rift somewhere.

I never knew an hour so drear

Love could not fill it full of cheer.

JOHN KENDRICK BANGS

LIGHTNING STRIKES TWICE

❈

Nobody knows the trouble I've seen.
Nobody knows my sorrow.
Nobody knows the trouble I've seen.
Nobody knows but Jesus!

NEGRO SPIRITUAL

I never had any question about what I wanted to do with my life. I would marry, major in advertising at the University of Minnesota, and then open my own ad agency.

Right out of college I tasted success. Soon my company was billing in the millions. I bought an airplane, a boat, a Mercedes, a limo. I entertained my clients at lavish dinners and events. There seemed to be no limit to my bank account. I married Karla. Everything was going according to plan.

Then desktop publishing arrived on the business scene—and disaster struck. I watched many of my clients depart as they opened their own in-house agencies. Slowly I began to lose financial ground, and the toys started to disappear. I sold my Mercedes and my Fiat on the same painful day, and four months later I watched as someone drove my limo away. Soon I was forced to find a buyer for my four-seater airplane and then, at last, my boat.

While the money had flowed, Karla and I had collected so many things, some useful, others useless. Now my wife recommended that we sell many of these possessions at weekend garage sales to cover our living expenses. "We don't really need them anyway," she declared.

It wasn't long until I was stripped of everything—except Karla. I figured soon she'd be disappearing too because most of my focus had been on money and not her.

Then, just when I figured things couldn't get much worse, they did. In the next six months, most of my staff left, taking chunks of the business with them. My wife and daughter were rushed to an emergency room after a near-fatal accident. My father died of cancer. And finally, our house was struck by lightning and, shortly after that, attacked by giant ants. (I'm not kidding!)

I felt like a modern-day Job. I'll never forget the day I came home from work feeling everything was at an end. I sat at the kitchen table, my face in my hands. All that remained was for Karla to leave.

But unlike Job's wife, who said, "Curse God and die!" Karla encouraged me. "Honey, I believe in you," she said. "And what's more, this is probably the best thing that has ever happened to us."

I looked at her as if she had lost her mind. But that was the turning point. The years that followed proved she was right.

Today, Karla and I view our past adversities as a valuable learning experience—not a hard-luck story. All those losses drew us closer together and closer to God. I gave up my fantasy that I could actually control the world. And with Karla's sweet help, I learned all over again how to enjoy simple pleasures in life—the smell of toothpaste on my child's breath at bedtime, the sight of a single flower in our garden, my wife's loving touch on my arm.

I always thought that the "poorer" in "for richer or poorer" was something terrible a spouse promised to endure. But now I know the truth. Less is often more. And a husband's true riches are best measured by how much love remains when everything else is taken away.

STEVE GOTTRY

ome couples begin marriage extremely poor and extremely happy. And through the years, some of those same couples gain a great measure of prosperity...but add to their happiness nothing at all.

Cars and homes and furnishings are nice, toys and boats and RVs are fun, stock portfolios and mutual funds give a pleasant illusion of security...but where did the laughter go? Where's the spontaneity? Where are those times of leaning on each other, covering for each other, crying with each other, and depending on each other as if there were no tomorrow?

Wealthy or poor, a husband and wife must find again those things that made them rich in joy, rich in adventure, rich in the delight of one another.

When the well is dry, we know the worth of water.

BENJAMIN FRANKLIN

It is astonishing how little one

feels poverty when one loves.

JOHN BULWER

A CHRISTMAS REMEMBERED

∞

Heap on more wood!—The wind is chill;
But let it whistle as it will.
We'll keep our Christmas merry still.

SIR WALTER SCOTT

'd known Beth all my life, but it wasn't until I ran into her after college that we fell in love.

I was thrilled when she agreed to marry me, especially in light of my career plans. Immediately following our wedding, we flew to Japan, where I intended to study the Japanese language in anticipation of becoming an international lawyer. I could offer Beth no white picket fence, at least not for a while.

Japan was exciting for me, but for Beth, who had never been away from home, it was a difficult adjustment. She knew no Japanese and couldn't find a job. Our apartment was smaller than the bathroom we have today! Even though Beth was a great sport about it all, I knew she was very lonely and homesick.

Late that fall Beth's spirits seemed to lift as she began planning our first Christmas together. She busily made ornaments, centerpieces, and stockings. "I'm going to make our first Christmas the most memorable ever!" she proclaimed.

When I came home each night, she'd proudly display a new Christmas ornament for our tree. She was so happy about them I didn't have the heart to tell her there were no Christmas trees in Japan! In fact, it was against Japanese law to cut down trees.

As the season drew closer, I began praying every day for a Christmas tree for my wife. "Nothing is impossible with God," I reminded myself. I asked everyone I knew or met if they could help me. I tracked down every lead I was given, but I couldn't produce a single tree.

One night Beth announced that she was ready for her tree, and I was finally forced to explain there wouldn't be one. My sweet wife was so gracious about the news. But I could see the disappointment in her eyes even as she declared, "We'll still have a wonderful Christmas!"

Christmas Eve found me dejected about the tree, but I was also happily anticipating the evening with my Beth. When I got off the bus, I began to run toward our apartment. Yes, I was going home empty-handed, but I was going home to the most wonderful wife in the whole world!

Then I saw it. At first I rubbed my eyes to make sure I wasn't hallucinating. There in the gutter was a beautiful Christmas tree, tinsel still sparkling in its branches! Surely someone had thrown it away. But how could that be, since it was Christmas Eve?

I scooped up the tree and took it home to my bride. Beth squealed with delight when she greeted me at the door. It was a miracle!

After eating the delicious dinner Beth had prepared, we spent the evening decorating our tree and marveling together over God's kindness to us. We kept the tree up as long as we could, discarding it only after it became a fire hazard.

Today we live in America, and getting a Christmas tree is as easy as a trip to the woods or the supermarket. But we've never found another tree quite as beautiful as that first one. Beth was right. Our first Christmas was the most memorable ever.

FRED BLUMER

⁂

This is Christmas:
not the tinsel, not the giving and receiving,
not even the carols, but the humble heart that
receives anew the wondrous gift, the Christ.

FRANK McKIBBEN

Love is the most terrible, and also the most generous of the passions; it is the only one that includes in its dreams the happiness of someone else.

J. A. KARR

In Sickness and in Health

arriage is a relationship between two eternal souls temporarily housed in fragile, failing bodies. Solomon, who knew a few things about marriage, once wrote: "Two are better than one, because they have a good return for their work: If one falls down, his friend can help him up. But pity the man who falls and has no one to help him up!" (Ecclesiastes 4:9–10).

Marriage says, "No matter what…"

"No matter what happens to you, I will be there at your side."

"No matter what you must endure, be it pain, or dread, or weakness, or sorrow, or loss, or indignity, I will endure with you. I am one with you."

"No matter what path you must walk, however long, however dark, however difficult, you will not walk it alone."

And things can never go badly wrong,

If the heart be true and the love be strong,

For the mist, if it comes, and the weeping rain

Will be changed by the love if not sunshine again.

GEORGE MACDONALD

UNFORGETTABLE LOVE

❦

Thou art my life, my love,
My heart, the very eyes of me,
And hast command of every part
To live and die for thee.

Sir Walter Scott

The old man slips out of his jacket and Ivy League cap and into the routine. "How're we doing today, mother?" he asks the woman in the wheelchair.

He pauses just for and instant—expectantly, as if she might actually answer him—but as always she stares straight ahead without speaking or acknowledging his presence. He runs a hand gently through the close-cropped white hair and remembers a time when it was different: long, luxurious, the color of fire. A lifetime ago, when *everything* was different....

In the beginning, theirs was a forbidden alliance. Her staunch, Scotch-Irish father disapproved of the young, handsome Italian who had gone to work as a laborer right after grade-school to support his mother and five siblings after his own father's death. Yet, despite the obstacles the two of them faced (or perhaps because of them), their love bloomed. Wanting desperately to be together, they stole away one night and found a sympathetic priest to marry them.

In due time they were blessed with a son (the image of his father) and a daughter (the image of Shirley Temple). Having secured a steady job with the local gas company to provide for his family, he had earned the respect of the community (and, at last, his father-in-law), and life was good.

But life doesn't always stay that way, and one spring afternoon in 1944 tragedy struck. Walking home from school through an alley with her brother, "Little Sister" (age six) was hit by a truck and killed. He was forced to assume the grim task of identifying his daughter's body; his wife was much too distraught. On the brink of despair, she withdrew from the world. But he, ever the strong one, cajoled her into going about the business of living again. God blessed them with more children: another son and daughter, fourteen months apart. And, though they would never completely forget the pain of loss, happiness once more filled their home.

Happiness and heartache—over the years they would have their share of both. The sorrow of sending a son off to war; the joy of welcoming him back. The horror of having their remaining daughter badly injured in an accident; the pulling together as a family as they helped her convalesce. And then there were the weddings, the children-in-law they would embrace as their own, the arrival of grandchildren and, eventually, great-grandchildren—and through it all they cherished each other with the same unwavering devotion as when they first fell in love.

Knowing she'd always hated her given name—Armenta—he had taken to calling her "mother" almost as soon as she became one. And though she sometimes called him "dad" for the benefit of the children in her heart, he would always be "Jimmy," a term of endearment reminiscent of their shared youth. Jimmy. It was possibly the last word she ever said—in her final lucid moment, before the cruel affliction known as Alzheimer's robbed her of her memory and her speech.

Occasionally some well-meaning person would question him about his daily pilgrimage to the home, where his uncommon faithfulness had made him something of a legend.

"Why do you do it, day after day? She doesn't even know who you are."

And his answer was always the same: "Maybe not. But I know who she is."

As he looks into her dark, shining eyes, the only vestiges of the woman she used to be (his wife, his partner, his dearest friend), he searches for a sign that perhaps on some level she still recognizes him. But, finding no such sign, he sighs.

"What do you say, Mother? Are you ready to eat?"

And, as he has done every morning for the past five years, he tenderly fastens a bib around her neck and begins to feed her breakfast.

MARY JEANNET LEDONNE

In loving memory of my father-in-law, James V. LeDonne, who passed away on December 8, 1997.
He was utterly devoted to my mother-in-law for the nearly sixty-six years they were married.

Grant that I may

not so much

seek to be loved

as to love.

For it is in giving

that we receive.

ST. FRANCIS OF ASSISI

Love is an

irresistible desire

to be irresistibly

desired.

ROBERT FROST

There are places in the heart where you don't wear muddy shoes. You enter carefully. You walk quietly. You speak softly.

These are the treasure rooms…the places where you keep all that you hold valuable and precious. A woman needs to know that her husband keeps her portrait on the wall of that room, where the morning light reaches through the window with the first caress of dawn. A man, too, needs to know that his wife esteems him above all others.

Other objects will seek to force entry into those treasure rooms…untimely, unworthy things that don't belong. (Do you stack old newspapers in a temple?) If a person isn't careful, the rooms may become nothing more than dusty storerooms, filled with things once desired, but now valued little.

Only cherished things belong in such places of the heart. And that is where a man ought to keep his wife and life companion. Right there, in that high and holy place just below (but never higher than) the place reserved for God. And that wife must hold her husband dearer than houses or wealth or career or even children.

We honor that which we cherish.

We protect that which we cherish.

We guard and prize and treasure that which we cherish.

Marriage says, "I cherish you, my love, most of all."

IF I SPEAK IN THE TONGUES OF MEN AND OF ANGELS,

BUT HAVE NOT LOVE, I AM ONLY A RESOUNDING

GONG OR A CLANGING CYMBAL.

IF I HAVE THE GIFT OF PROPHECY AND CAN FATHOM

ALL MYSTERIES AND ALL KNOWLEDGE, AND IF I

HAVE A FAITH THAT CAN MOVE MOUNTAINS, BUT

HAVE NOT LOVE, I AM NOTHING.

IF I GIVE ALL I POSSESS TO THE POOR AND SURRENDER

MY BODY TO THE FLAMES, BUT HAVE NOT LOVE, I

GAIN NOTHING.

Love is patient,
     love is kind.
It does not envy,
     it does not boast,
it is not proud.
     It is not rude,
it is not self-seeking,
     it is not easily angered,
it keeps no record of wrongs.
     Love does not delight in evil
but rejoices with the truth.
     It always protects,
always trusts,
     always hopes,
always perseveres.
     Love never fails.

1 CORINTHIANS 13:1-8

THE GARDEN OF LOVE

∞

Live now, believe me, wait not till tomorrow;
Gather the roses of life today.

PIERRE DE RONSARD

Before I met my husband, John, every attempt I'd made to find and keep love had led to disappointment and heartbreak.

John knew this, and so when he proposed to me, he vowed, "Your life with me will be a bed of roses!"

I was deeply touched by John's sentiment, especially since I knew he would do everything he could to make good on his promise. But of course, hardships come in life no matter how wonderfully our spouses treat us. And by the time our tenth anniversary rolled around, we'd experienced our share of stress and difficulty. It had been the hardest year we'd encountered together so far. What if John actually forgot our anniversary? After all, I'd been disappointed by men so many times before.

I needn't have worried. John took me to a beautiful restaurant where he'd reserved a table with a lovely view. After a delicious, romantic meal by candlelight, we returned home and prepared for bed. In our bathroom, I brushed my hair a long time and applied some of John's favorite perfume.

When I came back into the bedroom, I noticed that John was smiling like an excited little boy. I couldn't imagine what he'd been up to. Then suddenly he folded back the bedcovers, and I gasped with delight and surprise. The entire bed was covered in rose petals, their fragrance filling the room.

"John, how did you do this? Where did you get all these roses?"

"Well," he said with a big grin, "I called the florist and ordered pale pink Oceana roses like the ones you carried in your bouquet when we married. I requested that the blossoms be full and that the roses not be arranged. Then I spent hours gently pulling the petals apart."

I was so overwhelmed by his gesture that my eyes spilled over with tears.

As John kissed them away, he gently held me and whispered, "Didn't I promise you a bed of roses when I proposed?"

"Yes, you did! But I never…"

That evening John and I celebrated our anniversary in a garden of love—and there were no thorns. I felt my wounded heart let go of old pains and lingering doubts. In their place, a healing peace engulfed me, and I fully understood the words from 1 John 4:18 (NASB) for the first time: "Perfect love drives out fear."

ANN PLATZ

∞

Sweetheart, come see if the rose
Which at morning began to unclose
Its damask gown to the sun.
Has not lost, now the day is done,
The folds of its damasked gown
And its colors so like your own.

PIERRE DE RONSARD

They that love beyond the world

cannot be separated by it.

WILLIAM PENN

Love between two children of God outlives the union, outlives failing bodies, outlives the earth itself. Love, in whatever celestial form it takes in heaven, lives on after the earthly shell has passed into dust.

For the one who believes, death changes "good-bye" into other, more hopeful words.

I will see you soon, my love. I cannot bring you back to me, but I can come to you.

And I will.

Sleep on, beloved sleep,

and take thy rest;

Lay down thy head

upon thy Savior's breast.

We love thee well,

but Jesus loves thee best.

Good night!

Good night!

Good night!

SARAH DOUDNEY

LOVE LETTER FROM HEAVEN

∞

What greater thing is there for two human souls
than to feel that they are joined…
to strengthen each other…
to be at one with each other in silent
unspeakable memories.

GEORGE ELIOT

Several years ago my husband, George, died of complications following an automobile accident. Ours had been a long, happy marriage, and his death left me deeply depressed. As time passed, instead of being grateful for all the wonderful years we'd shared, I became engulfed in self-pity. Often I prayed, "Lord, why didn't you take me first?"

When I broke my leg a few weeks before my ninetieth birthday, I felt more confined—and alone—than ever. "If only George were here," I despaired, "he would chase away this sadness with words of wisdom and encouragement."

On this particularly blue day, I decided to call a friend and ask her to visit. Unfortunately, she was leaving on a trip and couldn't come.

I understood. But as I hung up the phone, tears started to flow. I moved to the window to sit in my favorite chair with Duke, my beloved cat, curled up in my lap. "Dear God," I prayed, weeping, "please give me the strength to get through this hour."

Get your Bible, a quiet voice inside me nudged. But my Bible was in the bedroom, and with my leg in a cast, it would be too hard to retrieve. Then I remembered my small travel Bible. Hadn't I seen it in the living room bookshelf? I found it and opened it, surprised to discover that it was George's old travel Bible instead of mine. They looked alike, and I thought I'd given his Bible away.

I turned the pages until I reached my favorite Scripture. Suddenly a letter fell into my lap. Carefully I unfolded the yellowed pages. It was a love letter from George. In it, he expressed his deep affection for me. His words of comfort went straight to my lonely heart.

My cheeks wet with tears, I continued to leaf through the Bible. In the back pages I found more notes from George. According to the date, he'd written these in the hospital prior to an earlier surgery. He must have feared that he would not return home. After he recovered from the surgery, the letter and notes were forgotten.

But no, I realized. They were *never* forgotten. God knew exactly where George's words of comfort were hidden—and exactly when I'd need them the most. Laughing some and crying some, I spent the rest of the afternoon basking in the company of both my husband and my Lord. I never felt less alone, and now I knew for certain that I never would be.

LUCILLE HEIMRICH

My Dearest Lucille,

I just wanted to let you know how much I care for you. I haven't always been a perfect husband but you've always loved me—imperfections and all. Since the day we met I have continued to love you more and more.

I thank God for each day He has allowed me to be with you. I don't know if I'm going to make it this time, but I do know that if I have to leave, I will have lived a wonderful life. You can know that I will always be with you, whether in this life or in the next.

In deepest Love

Your George

The minute I heard my first love story
I started looking for you,
not knowing how blind that was.
Lovers don't finally meet somewhere.
They're in each other all along.

RUMI

But there's nothing

half so sweet in life

as love's young dream.

THOMAS MOORE